Learning How to Say You Are Sorry

Susan Kent

The Rosen Publishing Group's
PowerKids Press™
New York

For Maris

Published in 2001 by The Rosen Publishing Group, Inc.
29 East 21st Street, New York, NY 10010

First Edition

Book Design: Maria E. Melendez

Photo Credits: Cover and title page pp. 4, 7, 8, 11, 12, 15, 16, 19, 20 by Debra Rothstein-Brewer.

Kent, Susan, 1942–
     Learning how to say you are sorry / by Susan Kent.
        p. cm.— (The violence prevention library)
     Includes index.
     Summary: Describes a variety of mistakes, such as breaking something, hurting someone's feelings, or being disobedient, and the importance of apologizing for them.
     ISBN 0-8239-5614-8
     1. Apologizing—Juvenile literature. [1. Apologizing.] I. Title. II. Series.

BF575 .A75 K46 2000
158.2—dc21   99-056859

Manufactured in the United States of America

Contents

Everyone Makes Mistakes

Everyone makes mistakes. Some are small. Other mistakes are big and can cause trouble. Since everyone makes mistakes, try not to feel bad about yourself when you make them. Instead say you are sorry, and try not to make the same mistake again.

It can be hard to admit you made a mistake. You might feel **embarrassed** and worry that people will be angry with you. Just as you want praise when you do things well, you have to accept the **consequences** of your mistakes. Mistakes are not all bad, though. They can help you learn and grow.

◀ *This girl feels bad because she broke her toy by mistake.*

Marty and Amy

Marty is supposed to watch his sister, Amy, at the park. He decides to play ball with his friends. He tells Amy to sit and watch them play. Marty has a great time and forgets to check on his sister. When the game ends, he cannot find Amy. Marty is worried. He looks everywhere. Finally he finds Amy sitting on a curb crying. She tried to go home but lost her way. Marty tells Amy he is sorry for not taking care of her. Marty also tells his parents he is sorry. When they punish him, he knows he deserves it. Marty is just glad that Amy is okay.

Marty is sorry that he did not take good care of his sister. ▶

Saying You Are Sorry

When you admit you did something wrong, you take the first step in learning from your mistake. The next step is saying you are sorry to anyone who is hurt by what you did wrong. If you tease your friends and hurt their feelings, **apologize**. Just saying you are sorry is not enough, though. You need to feel sorry, too. When you **regret** what you did, your apology will be **sincere**. This will help make the people you hurt feel better. They will also be more likely to **forgive** you. When you say you are sorry and mean it, you will feel better, too.

Saying you are sorry is important when you have made a mistake.

9

Showing You Are Sorry

The last step in learning from your mistakes is to try to make up for them. If you break someone's toy, you can offer to replace it. This shows that you are sorry. Sometimes, though, no matter how hard you try, you cannot make up for what you did wrong. If you spill paint on a classmate's drawing, nothing can take the paint away. Sometimes it is impossible to make up for your mistakes. By saying you are sorry, you let people know you care. You show them that you realize you have done something wrong. You show **respect** for their feelings.

Helping to fix something you have broken is a good way to show you are sorry.

10

Saying You Are Sorry at Home

Tell your family you are sorry when you do something wrong. When you are in a bad mood, you might call your sister names. You might refuse to do whatever your baby-sitter asks. You might even yell at your mom and dad. What will happen then? Everyone will be in a bad mood!

To make your family members feel better, apologize. Tell your sister you are sorry. Do something nice for your baby-sitter who takes such good care of you. Give your mom and dad a hug. If you do, your home can be a happier place.

◀ *It is a nice idea to give your mom a hug after you say you are sorry.*

When You Are Mean

Sometimes we do the wrong thing on purpose and then regret it later. You might get angry with your brother and hide his baseball glove. You might join friends in teasing someone who you think is different. When you think about it, you will probably start to feel bad. No one likes getting teased. When you do something mean, you may tell yourself that it does not matter. It does matter. Not only have you hurt someone else, you have hurt yourself, too. When we behave badly, we lose our **self-respect**.

Teasing someone can make you feel bad about yourself, too. ▶

Rosa and Kate

Rosa plays with Kate, a new neighbor, all summer. When school starts, Rosa wants to hang out with her old friends. When Kate says "Hi" in the halls, Rosa ignores her. Later, she sees Kate walking home looking sad. Rosa feels **ashamed**. She tells Kate she is really sorry. She asks her to forgive her. Rosa invites Kate to eat lunch with her the next day. She introduces Kate to her other friends. Kate is glad Rosa apologized and is happy to be included. Rosa also feels good inside. She keeps her new friend, her old friends, and her self-respect.

◀ *When Rosa apologizes to Kate, she makes Kate happy. Rosa feels better about herself, too.*

17

Saying You Are Sorry at School

If you want to have, and keep, friends, always tell them you are sorry when you do something that hurts them. At school, be sure to apologize to your classmates if you do something to upset them. It is also important to say you are sorry to your teacher if you cause trouble in class. You can also let your classmates and teacher know that you feel sorry when something bad happens to them, even when you had nothing to do with it. They will be grateful for your kindness. You will feel good, too. Your school will be a better place for everyone.

If you do something wrong in class, you should apologize to your teacher. ▶

Alicia and Billy

When a group of kids tease Soo Ling because of her accent, Alicia tells her she is sorry they are so mean. When Habib is knocked down in the hallway, Billy apologizes for the bullies. Alicia and Billy try to get their classmates to stop being mean. When that does not work, they decide to form a school club. They make posters saying "Be Nice" and "Different—Yes!" They get their classmates to sign a **pledge** saying they will treat others with respect. Thanks to their efforts, their school is a safer, happier place. Soon everyone feels like they belong there.

◄ *Forming a club is a good way to help teach others about respect.*

Feeling Proud of Yourself

Since you, and everyone else, will make mistakes all your life, you will have plenty of chances to say you are sorry. Remember to admit when you do something wrong. Then say you are sorry. Finally, show you mean it by trying to fix the problem. When you do these things, you make the people around you feel good and you earn their respect. These small steps add up and help make your world a better place. You can feel very proud of yourself.

Glossary

apologize (uh-PAH-lo-jyz) To tell someone you are sorry.

ashamed (uh-SHAYMD) To feel bad because you have done something wrong.

consequences (KON-suh-kwen-sez) Things that happen as a result of something you did.

embarrassed (im-BAYR-ist) Feeling uncomfortable or ashamed.

forgive (FOHR-giv) To no longer be angry with someone who did something wrong to you.

pledge (PLEJ) A promise or agreement.

regret (REE-gret) To feel sorry about doing something. To wish you had never done it.

respect (ree-SPEKT) To think highly of someone or something.

self-respect (SELF-ree-SPEKT) To think highly of yourself.

sincere (sin-SEER) To be honest about one's feelings.

Index